A Murmuration of Starlings

Crab Orchard Series in Poetry
OPEN COMPETITION AWARD

T0164374

A Murmuration of Starlings

JAKE ADAM YORK

Crab Orchard Review

&

Southern Illinois University Press

CARBONDALE

11   10   4   3   2

The Crab Orchard Series in Poetry is a joint publishing venture of
Southern Illinois University Press and *Crab Orchard Review*. This series has
been made possible by the generous support of the Office of the President
of Southern Illinois University and the Office of the Vice Chancellor for
Academic Affairs and Provost at Southern Illinois University Carbondale.

Crab Orchard Series in Poetry Editor: Jon Tribble
Open Competition Award Judge for 2007: Cathy Song

Library of Congress Cataloging-in-Publication Data
York, Jake Adam.
    A murmuration of starlings / Jake Adam York.
       p. cm. — (Crab Orchard series in poetry)
    ISBN-13: 978-0-8093-2837-6 (alk. paper)
    ISBN-10: 0-8093-2837-2 (alk. paper)
    I. Title.

PS3625.0747M86   2008
811'.6—dc22   2007031729

Printed on recycled paper. ♻

The paper used in this publication meets the minimum requirements
of American National Standard for Information Sciences—Permanence of
Paper for Printed Library Materials, ANSI Z39.48-1992. ∞

Cover photo: By Bob Adelman. Birmingham, Alabama, 1963. Firemen
turn high-powered hoses, capable of stripping bark from trees, against
peaceful demonstrators, who are knocked down and skid across the grass
in Kelly Ingram Park. By coming together and holding on to one another,
the demonstrators are able to stand up to the fire hoses. When the firemen
found they could no longer knock down the united protestors, they turned
off their hoses.

No lie can live forever.

—MARTIN LUTHER KING JR.

Contents

Acknowledgments

Grateful acknowledgment is made to the editors of the following publications where some of these poems appeared, sometimes in slightly different form:

Blackbird — "For Lamar Smith," "At Liberty" (Lee),
   "Substantiation," and "For Reverend James Reeb"
Cannibal — "At Money"
DIAGRAM — "The Crowd He Becomes"
New South — "Shall Be Taught to Speak," "A Murmuration of
   Starlings," "March," and "Watch"
Handsome — "Tuck"
Memorious — "At Liberty" (Allen)

Thanks to my friends and interlocutors who helped these poems rise into hearing, especially Dan Albergotti, Aaron Anstett, Hadara Bar-Nadav, Scott George Beattie, Diann Blakely, Simmons Buntin, Chris Campagna, Bill Cobb, Matthew Cooperman, Greg Donovan, Mary Flinn, Janis Frame, Gina Franco, Noah Eli Gordon, Matt Henriksen, Major Jackson, Rodney Jones, David Keplinger, Alex Lemon, Adam Lerner, Maurice Manning, Elliott McPherson and the Dexateens, Robert Morgan, Jim Murphy, Joshua Poteat, Elizabeth Robinson, Jenny Sadre-Orafai, Zachary Schomburg, Sarah Skeen, Dave Smith, R. T. Smith, Mathias Svalina, Joshua Marie Wilkinson, Susan Settlemyre Williams, and my students who were, sometimes, the first to see drafts of these poems.

And special gratitude to my family, for their understanding, their support, their stories, and their teaching.

A Murmuration of Starlings

Shall Be Taught to Speak

March 1890

> I'll have a starling shall be taught to speak
> Nothing but "Mortimer," and give it him
> To keep his anger still in motion.
>   —*Henry IV*, Part One

Schieffelin's cages champ the morning air.
Forty hands on the latches wait for the sign.

Dawn invades, feathering trees he's civilized
with sparrows, finches, a failure of nightingales,

and now the least of Shakespeare's birds,
forty pairs of starlings for the New World's nests.

Even he cannot know how they'll explode,
how they'll plume, then pair, then spread

to double, a hundred, two hundred million
in a century, maybe more, how they'll swallow

all the country's wandering songs
then speak their horrors from the eaves.

A thousand miles away, in Arkansas,
six men pose beneath a tree. In the photograph,

the hanged man's sweater's buttoned tight,
his hat, his head raked to hide the noose.

One man stills the body with his cane.
Another moves to point, but his arm is blurred.

Trees burn quietly in the morning sun.
Their jaws are set. Just one thing's in motion.

For Lamar Smith

13 August 1955, Brookhaven, Mississippi

No one sees him cross the courthouse lawn,
the lone black man in the election crowd,

and no one steps from the line and pulls a gun
then slips past the sheriff and the whole white town

and no one disappears into history
covered in blood and gunpowder sulphur

while the old man collapses in wreathes of smoke
and ballots wing in the billow of his fall.

Townsfolk stand in a cigarette cloud, the dead man
under their breath half nightmare, half dream,

heat shimmer wind could blow away.
The poll-list crackles as they break.

Ashes feather from his wounds.
Like smoke from their mouths when they say the word.

At Liberty

21 September 1961, Liberty, Mississippi

Everyone will say he drove to the gin
with a truck full of cotton so he drives to the gin
and gets in line and everyone will say
the congressman pulled in behind him so he gets out
yelling *Herbert Lee I'm not messing with you this time*
and his affidavit will say Lee had a tire iron
and there are no photographs so there is
a tire iron and since the congressman will say
Lee swung at him his hand will grasp the iron
under the tangle of his own dead weight
and the congressman will leave and will not
see him again so he just lies there bleeding
and no one will touch him so for a time
he is just a story or a huddle of starlings
or crows or a cloud of bottle-flies that might
explode and disappear until the witnesses
can say he's there and an undertaker can come
with a hearse from the next county over
and then he is dead and the congressman can
tell his story so Herbert Lee will rise
from his coffin and swing his iron
and the FBI can come to make him into evidence
but someone will have roped him into his grave
so there is no photograph and no one sees
the cotton boll wicking blood so there is no boll
only a clear, white negative in the dark
and a paper that slowly fills with flies.

Substantiation

And the way the jury chose to believe the ridiculous stories of the defense. . . .
    —Mamie Till, 1955

. . . with truth absent, hypocrisy and myth have flourished. . . .
    —*Look*, January 1956

The sheriff says it wasn't Till we pulled from the river,
that man was as white as I am, white as cotton
blowed by the cotton gin fan that weighed him down,
looked like he'd lain there weeks, not a kid at all.
He was a stranger just out of Money, recalled
by a store clerk, a hobo, and a crossroad guitarist.
The reporter finds them at the once abandoned crossing.
They say it's like the sheriff says, came up one night,
headed Clarksdale way, another one, hat pulled down,
right behind. Three days later, the bluesman says,
a plague of starlings gathered into little boys
those who fished and found the dead man's foot.
The reporter stares into his cataracted, cotton eyes.
He cannot find them, no matter where he looks.

*

The sheriff says this man's killer is on the loose
and a killer emerges, a child watching from a sleeping porch
catches a rustle in the bushes and soon everyone
is on the hunt while in the courtroom someone
is wondering about this poor murdered's family,
who's missing him, and the next day his father appears
unknown for work, his name on the payroll,
then gets to work at a machine no one's ever seen,
and someone is weeping on the Tallahatchie's bank,
a little girl who wished her mother would die,
whose mother died at the hands of this stranger
she's followed till he stepped in the river and disappeared.

*

The reporter asks for Too-Tight Collins at Charlestown jail
and the sheriff says Who? The reporter asks why he's got him
then sees the bullet on his tongue. Asks directions back
to Greenwood and finds himself down Greenville way instead.
Takes back roads back to Mound Bayou, wrong wrong turn
to Parchman Farm where guards rifle from the woods.
A change at the Eavesdrop Inn then he's bent picking cotton
in a field. Come sundown, he hobos Sumner way and squats
at courthouse windows where the sheriff shuffles cards
for a blind man and the defense team. At a levee camp that night
he asks for whiskey and she gives him a cup of names.
He wires his paper that he's gone catfish fishing
on the Tallahatchie, that he won't be coming home.

*

The defense says Till's alive and well on Detroit streets
and someone's sure they've seen him, just off the train
from Memphis, porters sneaking him out the back
and now he's walking incognito, a worn fedora raked
to shade the one eye. A cruiser eases through the streets,
searchlight in doorways, the driver white,
dressed like a cop but for the rope marks at his throat,
the bullet in his eye. He has a mushmouth accent,
talks water when he speaks, slept in a box from Greenville
to Chicago with another man's name, a name
he's ready to give up now. If Till is alive and well,
he can't rest in Burr Oak Cemetery, will cruise
where he's been said to be on the Detroit streets
where everyone knows he's coming
since he whistles like a train on the way out of town.

*

They say it was darker than a thousand midnights
in the cabin, they couldn't find him in the dark.
They say that Moses brought him out at last,
that someone else was in the truck to say
that it was him that did the talk at Money.
They say they took him for a ride, to rough him up,
scare him on a river bluff then let him go.
They say they let him off near Glendora,
never seen again. They say Ain't it like a negro
to swim the river with a gin fan round his neck.
They say it was hog's blood in the truck
what Too Tight washed. They say
they never burnt no shoes, it was a barbecue.
They say Too Tight never worked for them,
they never heard of Willie Reed. They say
they never meant to harm the boy, they didn't do a thing.

*

The defense says Mamie Till knows her son's
alive and well, that she knows the body isn't his.
That her lawyers came in weeks ago and dug a body up
and used it for their own. That they've found fresh graves.
That a Yazoo City widow found her husband's gone
and Lazarus ain't walking back through Eden,
Greenwood, Itta Bena. That Jesus Christ ain't come.
Every Leflore County lawyer can't be wrong.
One juror says he knows it, seen rights workers
take their shovels out along the roads at night.
That Sheriff Strider's right. That it's the northern poison
got this all stirred up. That though a black might be
fool enough to swim with a gin fan round his neck,
this one wasn't one. That they should sit a while
and drink a pop, to make it look right, look real.

*

In the nervous ward, Reed remembers Milam with the gun
asking did he hear anything. Reed remembers saying no,
he didn't hear anything, anything. Remembers not hearing
the beating and the crying in the shed behind Milam's.
Remembers not thinking, they beatin' someone up there.
Remembers not passing the shed, not hearing the beating.
Remembers not remembering Milam not coming out,
not asking if he'd heard. Remembers not
not remembering on the stand, not not whispering
the court reporter not not recording his not
not remembered memory. Not not getting on the train.
Not hearing anything, anything. Such quiet now.

*

Now hypocrisy can be exposed; myth dispelled.
    —*Look*, January 1956

The reporter hears Bryant's been bragging
how he got away with murder. A few months back
no one could make them, and now they're seen
at the cabin, at the bridge, their alibis are gone.
The stranger emerges from the river then disappears.
The little girl's mother rises from her grave, home
just in time for dinner. Emmett Till boards a freight
in Detroit and hobos to his grave outside Chicago.
The crossroads station and its clerk disappear again
and the hat disappears. Anywhere else, the reporter
would have been called to the disappearing,
but here there's nothing left to say. Bryant's smile
broadens as he retells it, how they were heroes,
how they murdered Till. When the *Look* comes out,
the town already knows. No one ever speaks to them again.

*

When the contractor guts the courthouse basement,
the fan and the transcript are laid out on the street.
Junkmen salvage metal, and the papers warp and tear
in the rain. Starlings pick through the gutters' wreck
and weave typescript fragments into their nests.
Emmett Till watches, enwreathes their broods.
Milam wakes up early each morning when the riot
in the pear trees begins, starlings wolf-whistling
for food, or just repeating what they've heard.
One pair has woven strips of *Look* Bryant spreads
throughout the woods. In twenty years no one's come.
He opens a shotgun on the starlings' calls each morning
and they spray like smoke or blood. But they regather
and whistle overhead and shit back shot as they fly.

At Money

Still hot so breath takes breath away.

Heat, heart forgets—air's bakelite plaque.

A rust, a red—to beat. Tires spray.

Gravel, then excitements shroud all sound.

Movements that still. Quiet called heat.

Birds weigh lines but cannot witness.

A fender's smooth. Bluegreen glass.

Or a *lady*'s curves. Dark. That.

Wets the whistle. Burns a body warm.

B/W

"Out of this World" — 1946
Terminal Station, Birmingham

They arrive as holes in the sky
space shows through,
darks that meteor then wing
in the scaffolds of the welcome sign.
Sonny gazes from a rail,
his robe now a zoetrope's
crawl of shadow and light,
a semaphore no engineer can read.
Porters tell the sudden dim,
one how hot iron crashed,
a third-shift crew blown
to smoke, blackbirds
cast from charred flesh,
one how a hanged man burned
till crows erupted in the smoke,
one how spacerocks blazed
clear sky then shattered
to a billion starlings.
Now they rattle
The Magic City's steel.
Like Bracken in the film,
when they hinge their mouths
another voice emerges.
And when they rise
sun wheels from Sonny's
tinfoil crown till stars
fletch each watcher,
porters, conductors now

constellated with other skies,
each one poised,
ready to fly.

"*Some Enchanted Evening*"—1949
Dynamite Hill, Birmingham

Night torn like a cloud,
rags shrapnelling twilight,

spray on cinematic windows
of darkened cars

someone watches, at last
lost in the ballfield's glow.

Now the streets are dark,
fans static like a radio

blocks away. The sticks
sweat in his waiting hands.

Como warms the console:
Some enchanted evening, someone

may be laughing, and soon
he'll throw his package

and then the ash, he thinks,
will be the only black.

*

Morning, children crowd
a man-wide clearing in the char,

a grass silhouette
that fills with birds.

He wakes, blocks away,
broadcast static of fact,

bacon crackling till crisp,
till his work is baritoned,

now news, and they've renamed
the neighborhood

after him. Coffee steams
its fuses, and through the window

he can see each fist of smoke
unbillowing to a starling

and soon the clothesline's full
and the gun is in his hand.

"Blueberry Hill" / "Smokestack Lightnin'"—1957
Fountain Heights, Birmingham

Three cigarettes each, Blossburg to Birmingham.
Now, Fountain Heights, ash leaves in early dark

then gathers as they wait on the curb,
Fats drifting from an open window:

The moon stood still—On Blueberry Hill—
And lingered until—My dream came true.

Tonight there is no moon, not yet,
and they're laid back, waiting for the lights to die,

the way they did on Dynamite Hill,
the way they've done since Christmas,

first outside the preacher's house, then
New Year's here where the dark is moving in.

When the trees begin to hush in the wind,
the fireman's out, the bomb is thrown,

and before the house lights
just like gold, all anyone can see

is the cherry of his smoke redden
as radios catch Wolf's *Fare thee well*

if I never see you no more,
faint laugh of tires, O, *don't you hear me cryin?*

Le Son Ra's "Hours After" b/w "Great Balls of Fire" —1958
Chicago

A plain black disc
in Sonny's hands. A Saturn.
Starling's sheen.
Son says the new man
thinks the place he wants to go.
The needle drops.
He's halfway there.
He tells the band how men
will climb through stars,
great fireballs' hearts,
where they'll hear a music
no human's ever known.
Then their minds will move.
Today, he says, is the shadow
of tomorrow. Tomorrow
everything will be clear.
Tonight, the stars are hot,
white, the horns are gleam.
There is one sun, Ra,
and he wears the planets
on his chest. The needle
lifts, then kicks away.
Beyond the floods,
sequins twinkle like a city
from miles away.

"Blue Velvet"—September 15, 1963
Birmingham

She nests the paper by the phone.

*

But how to say it, call it in?

*

Four white men outside the funeral home.

*

Dome light burns their faces in the night.

*

Blue-and-white sunk in the blur of 2 A.M.

*

Plate numbers tangle in that fist of paper.

*

Vinton trembles some Memphis station.

*

Arc lights, the whole night's moving.

*

Shadows bruise shadows. Crushed.

*

Policeman and crow-dark blue.

*

Vinton incandescent.

*

But nothing else has blown.

*

Girls chorus in the distance.

*

Then the glow, and the question's gone.

"Out of this World" —1963
Birmingham / New York City

One picture's just a shoe
raised from the basement's wreck,
patent scarred as a record's black,
weeping from a hand.
What needle could descend
into that sound?
Sonny's come so far.
A thousand miles away,
Coltrane spins on the player,
and he tells no one
when angels speak of love
they speak cosmic waves
so long no one can hear.
Slow press on the bottom key,
a note that holds for days.
Coltrane's on the verse again,
his sweet unfolding longer,
more notes, more waves
drawn from the ancient tune,
and Sonny thinks of Bracken
in the film, another voice
emerging, then plays over
Coltrane's reed, his clavoline
screaming to the streets.
Outside, dawn is spreading,
bruise as a starling's wings.
Birds gather on the lines.
Each mouth opens
its own unearthly sing.

The Crowd He Becomes

15 September 1963, Birmingham

Later he will say he did not do it,
he was home at breakfast, just ask the wife,
say they heard some radio preacher doing
love thy neighbor while birds filled up the yard.
Later, he will say he did not do it then tell
how he didn't, lean in close to say
if he would have done it it wouldn't have been
alone, he would have had a driver
and a man out west to phone in threats
to draw the cops away. They'd ease
through empty streets to plant their package
then glide away, their route thick with friends,
a thousand ways to disappear.

*

The DA will lean, will see his would have
dashboard-lit, driving Dynamite Hill,
headlights, radio dead. Would have
in the shotgun seat, sticks sweating in his grip,
shadow steering through the city's sleep.
Will see them driving, out before the paperboys,
ready to throw when the dark is right.
See him Christmas, few years back,
outside the preacher's house, thin fuse of cigarette,
newspaper spread on the bus protests.
See flash, shock push him from the dark,
burn his shadow where anyone could see.
Something dark in the lenses of the bottle trees.

*

The photographer spots him eyeing
the bombed-out church, minutes after,
a face he's seen before, flash on the shards
of phone-booths and broken windows
he'll follow through the horrid and the horrified
while the cops arrive, the state patrol arrives
with bayonets instead of hoses, bayonets
instead of dogs, while congregants arrive
between firemen and plainclothes Klansmen
and the children, the children arrive
and depart, and there, the smirk he'll follow
through uniforms and Sunday black,
into the park, then lose him as it fills.

*

Will stand in the blur of what arrives and wonder
where he could have gone. Whether he'd cut
toward the depot, through the railyards to wind back home,
or north through the nervous blocks, or circle back
for another view, maybe shadowed in a doorway,
japing in a storefront window, listening at a sandwich stand
while everyone is talking, his work on every tongue.
Maybe he could drift through the crush of lookers
in cigarette smoke, in the breath of many lungs,
common, innocuous, a cloud about to disappear.

*

Will stand imagining him split at each intersection,
now four of him working the city's riot,
one with a bomb in his Sunday *Herald*,
one with a gun hung out the window racing
to a segregation rally, one with a bullhorn
and a speech for the news if they want it right,
and one just waiting for some midnight's cool
when he can stand beneath the vacant windows
and search for that fire in the face of Christ
before driving out past the mills. On the ridge
he'll see Vulcan's torch is red, but not for them.
Shadows reel from the furnace sheds,
birds exploding, blown from molten light.

*

The mayor says all of us are victims, innocent victims.
The lawyer kills his radio. When folks ask later
who did it, the lawyer says I'll tell you who.
Who is everyone who talks of *niggers*. Who is everyone
who slurs to his neighbors and his sons. Everyone
who jokes about *niggers* and everyone
who laughs at the jokes. Everyone who's quiet,
who lets it happen. Now his voice flaps in the rafters
of the meeting hall, and everyone is quiet.
I'll tell you who did it, he says. We all did.

*

The photographer keeps his beat, past the crater
in the church foundation, through the park,
into the midday rush, just where he lost him.
In the darkroom, he kept arriving, his face
framed between elbows, caught in the thrall,
or his crewcut, his smile cropped by arms.
Now his haircut, half-rolled sleeve, cigarette lip,
his eye pass by a dozen times, and more.
He could be anyone, could be everyone
wandering the storefronts, spying behind his *News*.
The photographer follows each one, cocked
and ready to shoot, but his lens can't catch them all
so he just stands, tracing their paths,
he just stands, lost in the crowd he becomes.

At Liberty

Louis Allen, 31 January 1964, Liberty, Mississippi

The morning train is turning like a compass needle

now the night has folded all its schedules

in the stands of pine and cedar, all its innumerable wings,

and tomorrow he will be gone from the lumber-yards

and the farmhouse windows that semaphore like televisions

and the vacant hands of Herbert Lee

and the killer and the quiet of having never seen a thing.

Quietly now, while his truck is idling,

dark decides from all the county's limbs,

shattering into birds that shatter then collapse to his skin.

Beaks lace eardrum and eardrum, his cheeks, his tongue,

their obsidians needling for what he's seen,

what he would surely tell, so he won't have to see it,

so he won't have to whisper it, even once, ever again.

Tuck

What if there is nothing left to do
but wander the barren earth and pick the hard obsidian from the dirt
and tuck it into our breasts where our hearts used to be?
  —April Bernard, "Blackbird Bye Bye"

There is a sky and
there is a sky.

Two birds

converge
from different mornings.

Starlings, Shakespeare's
fine-etched mimics

echo
beat and beat,

collapse in glass.

  *

In a Birmingham hotel,
thin tick a Byzantine

of birds, wings
embroidered into wings.

Hands doze
on these collisions.

From above,
a reveille,

a bluebird's or
wren's, catbird's

holler tenoring
There is no more

good water
because the pond is dry.

August '27
on the record,

the technician sweats
as Jaybird's wail

and Jaybird's harp
twine and groove,

blows the acetate's curls
where they'll be swept,

fine as hair,
thrown from the window,

a smear in the blistering air.

*

Underfeathers,
dust,

a bird,

heart-small
and jeweled

as a fairy-tale
nightingale

cradled
in the lilies' blades.

Topaz, lapis.
Jade.

Onyx
or obsidian.

Half-shine
of some forgotten toy.

*

Filaments read our fingerprints,

quiver weak
to the wingbones' hollows.

The fine hairs of its feathers
breathe in our breathing,

feather in the close-up lens.

*

Subtone or
halftone warming

the saxophone's brass
lost in bass-

line, vamp,
applause.

A stillness, a tensing
that sounds like quiet,

Freedom Summer's
firebombs, knuckles,

pipes
about to land.

Now *there is nothing left*

but a needle
instead of a needle,

a needle cutting

*No one here who loves
and understands me*

in hard dark,
hard luck

shattered, glass,

Coltrane's reed

cutting an elsewhere
in the air

*

Cornell carving
towhees, junkos,

slenderest wrens,
the mockingbird

from field guides'
endplates, war

on the radio, slicing
the numbered legend,

the starling hid
behind a twig,

half silhouette,
parenthetic

as a beak
cracked like a seed,

a space in which
the notes can arrive

*

an ambulance,
an abandoned child,

dopplered ululation

lighting
on the telephone wire.

Whistle, ruffle.

Shovel, cough.

*

In the photograph, later,
lost in the grain.

Halftone blur,
brass.

Blanks
darken in the trays,

bright shrinks to comets,
to meteors,

stars
beading

Aquila, Corvus,
Sturnus,

Saturns and satellites.

Nebulae.
Galactic spray.

*

Razor each jet
of gas and light

until the fine hairs feather
in our breath,

fingerprints luster
gloss and oil.

Blade on blade
the wings are arranged

like the hands of the dead,

stitched like pages,
bound to a coat-hanger frame,

coat-hanger spine
and cage, a nest,

mangle of audiotape
for an inside.

*

Set it in the window
so wind might caress

when we cannot sleep.
When we cannot sleep

it twinkles like the night.

Starlings gather in the branches.

Names whisper from the sheen.

For Reverend James Reeb

9 March 1965, Selma, Alabama

The ministers rise from empty plates
like the steam of chicken and greens

and puff into coats, into prayers, and then
the unlit streets, ready for tomorrow's march

or gathering or prayers, and then the dark
is beating *Hey niggers* though only their coats are black

and the night and everything so they cannot see
what's coming, what hits them, what feet, what pipes

at their ribs, who's saying *Now you know,*
now you know what it's like to be a real nigger

and no one can see what lands, what cracks
the skull, the hairline fracture in tangled hair,

what's nesting, what's beating there,
what wings are gathering in his eyes.

A Murmuration of Starlings

for Jimmie Lee Jackson
18–26 February 1965, Marion and Selma, Alabama

A cloud of starlings drifts from the river,

at first, a smudge on the sky
or the hospital window,

then more definite,

contracting then scattering
like pain.

Nuns ghost, white-robed

as night riders in the farm-edge pines
haunting the forest along the river,

like lilies on Cahaba's shoals.

*

Whenever he wakes someone else is there
just out of view

prayer drowned in the rasp of breath

a song like breaking glass.

Wings clench in the fluorescent tubes,
flutter of shadows

the state patrol colonel
darkening the bed

handcuffs on the rail,
a warrant for a tongue.

Then wings,
blown smoke

gathering somewhere
just out of view.

*

At the church just after dark

hymns, then the night march
across the square

to sing through the jailhouse window
and February to their brother

who can hear them in their pews,
hear them descend

to the waiting mayor and police chief,
state troopers who bullhorn them back.

When the reverend kneels to pray,
one patrolman swings his club,

all the lights go down.

　　*

Photograph strobes
carve their bodies from the dark,

break and pucker of serge and wool
on arms boxed

to catch the blows,

nightsticks straight
from the flex of uniform sleeves

coats taut between the blades,
white helmets' gleam

and above, a heaven of breath
and steam and smoke from which

dark feathers
then spreads

coughing dense night air
at the cusp of the lens

carving through the barrel

to spread the shutters blind

*

No one sees the congregation scatter

or the troopers chase

to the river or church
or blockhouse café

No one sees the bottles flying
as they climb the stairs

or the bricks in the troopers' affidavits

No one sees the clubs

or the thousand starlings
smoking at the lights

No one sees the old woman
swinging Cokes on the troopers' heads

or falling from their sticks

or the old man lunging in their affidavits
or falling

or the young one, the grandson
step in to catch the blow

or take the gun

*

They see the flash and kickback

Jimmie Lee folding in the glass

of the cigarette machine

tube light halo, electric hum

Smoke feathers

singing glass

the grandfather's face arriving, arriving

in the intermittent light.

*

No one sees them drag him down the stairs
and into the street

but that is where they found him

No one sees them beat so hard
clubs splinter

skin and spit and blood
through the haze of breath, bodies' steam

spit half-syllables
that echo from the church face,

the courthouse, tangled strange

and having
found each other

whole

as if the refugees of bone and skin
and breath

gathered in the eaves
and hollows of the dark

coalesce
so their blows return

ghost wings at their ears

*

Blood beading arc-lights' flicker, feathertips of faint
in the road's warm pitch, wings' sheen and the splay

of fingers, starlings descending from the dark,
assembling in his mother's warmth, having learned

her hush-now timbre but saying things he can't make sense.

He keeps saying their recurring sentences, what he hears
in the whisper songs at the lips of his ears.

The doctors open him again, one last
bullet, infection nesting there.

The pavement warm beneath.
Pulse of footfall. Wings.

*

Dark beats in the overhead lights
till the room is night and sheen

that folds from stars
then sky

into Selma's oaks
and the girders of the bridge

and the churches' steeples,
and into all the pines

from there to Marion,

gathering in the stands
around the farm

where his grandfather
follows the preachers

back through the woods.

*

February silvers all their bruises.
Breath curls into the pines,

into the murmuring dim

and when they slow
everything is quiet

and he can see the towns,
the map forming on their lips.

And when they speak
he sees

their mouths are full of birds.

March

Day is halos welded in his eyes,
corrals where shadows cannot move.
But he doesn't need to see
daylight copper half-cropped fields
to know that blindness, metal spill
on the highway and the fallows,
moss and the water-oaks beyond.
Sweat on a dray mule's hinds.
Usually, night's slow failing,
wished forgetting, but now
dark shatters, snows in kites
and wings to fill the field beyond
and swamp abandoned rows.
Hours, wind plows that pulse.
It ticks like a flock of crows.
Then music, a congregation
rising, breaths from ready,
hymnbooks cracking in their ears.

Watch

1965

Haze laced with crow, the sky
marbles darker, slow negative
to Montgomery's gleam.
Now the governor feels
the imminence, breath filling
the highways as shadows
gather into storm, miles
and miles of protest, columns
slowly filing into town.
Coalescing, what he can't forget,
Selma's tear-gas fog, the riot
of bodies tangled in that white,
wounds, scars unfolding.
Now the clouds are pulsing,
dark as a plague of starlings.
When the first thunder cracks,
he smells the rain already.
Black water pearls the eaves.

The Small Birds of Sound

State of Alabama v. Robert E. Chambliss, 1977

When they come
filling the yard with their overheard,

broke-glass catastrophes of voice,
overcrowded party line,

he lets the screen door clap
to see them plume

then settle back to the fence,
aftershocks of crowd and wail.

When they come
he says again he was home at breakfast

radio preacher doing love thy neighbor
and then the bomb,

just ask the wife.
The silence

in the TV's cathode glow
slowly fills with questions

as starlings shutter light
then weigh the lines, voices

tangled in their claws.

*

They had him buying dynamite,
a case he says he passed along,

then the other's car behind the church,
four men dome-lit in early dark.

Now all they have is years
of brag and noise and alibi,

a quiet
in which the trail's confused.

At times it seemed he wasn't real,
that he was no one,

a story everyone had heard,
just not the end,

that he was different men,
one arm with a bomb,

another making calls
miles outside of town,

a fog, an exhalation,
scattering when seen.

*

When the niece appears,
long silence ready to break

into small birds of sound,
the court's held breath

when she steps into the box and says
how she heard them

at the table the night before
beneath the naked bulb,

thick with beer,
cards down and laughing

when he leans through the light
and says *Wait. Just wait.*

Come Sunday, they'll beg us
to let them segregate.

Then everything stills
and she sees the lights'

flicker slow
and the whole room dims.

What he said gathers
where she's said it

a cloud
beneath the tube-lights' beat

he breathes in,
a dark that nests

in the wreck of his mouth

*

Then the wife rises
from her couch

lord have mercy
pulls the curtains

and the girlfriends appear
without their alibis

and the neighbor
who saw the sticks appears

and the park
where water spread like angels

in the photographs of the hosed,
the beaten, the harassed,

the park slowly fills
with starlings,

iridescent wings
creeling silence,

a murmur, a congregation's rising
now a certain quiet's gone.

*

In Kilby, all he'll say
is he gave the dynamite,
he said the thing.

They'll have to find
the others on their own.

In another cell, someone's humming
We Shall Overcome.
Laughter down the line.

Quiet crowds his throat.

They see it pulsing there.

*

He can rise at night
once the singing stops,

and look out over Jenkins Creek,
a stream of cooling steel,

toward Montgomery,
Selma

where no bomb
could stop them coming

where they slept in open fields

and filled the marble steps
as Wallace eyed them through the blinds.

Some nights the ground is moving
beneath the clouds,

the earth,
their waiting bodies

their hard
black stone.

At Sun Ra's Grave

Birmingham, 2001

Now our god's dismantled,
iron arms, iron hands now laid away,
vacant head beside his vacant feet.
Vulcan, God of All the Fire
That Sleeps in Mountains,
now a brash of empty veins.
Now only broadcast towers
lance the night, their amber pulse
the city's only torches,
and below, where the terminal station
blazed 10,000 lights in welcome,
Birmingham: The Magic City,
now expressway scars the blank
and even the streets are gone
where you walked as *Herman,*
then *Sonny,* musician, mystic,
man from Saturn, in your tinfoil hat
and bedsheet robe, and even
the house is gone, the room
where you played by radio light,
slowly casting off your names.

*

Now derelicts keep the rails
from the furnaces to the dead West End.
They nest in boxcars and dance-hall doors
boarded up to keep the silence in.
They rattle *White* and *Colored* signs
from scrapheaps and campfire on the slag.
They drift, split in lunchcounter windows
then crossing on streetcorners
where firemen hosed the marchers down,
attack dogs gnashing at their heels.
In Kelly Ingram Park, they haunt
bronze water cannons, bronze children
washed in sodium light. They rake
the teeth of cut-steel pinschers,
praying change from their metal tongues.
One lies beneath a swayback boy
hung in a bronze policeman's grip.
Dew rises through the halflight,
a gauze, departing wings.

＊

One drifts in the neon glow of the church's sign,
News wrapped tight around him. In the fold
below his shoulder, the Blanton trial is winding down,
the bomber abandoned, given up by his son,
ex-wife, and neighbors, tapes that have him saying
They ain't going to catch me when I bomb my next church.
In this light he can see the steps where they hid the sticks
are gone, the stained-glass face of Christ,
raised from shards now glows, its angle
an aftermath. But the rush, the wind's still here.
Wet night air spreads name from name,
pulling the sheets from his grip, high into the night.

*

Papers wing through the creosote dim,
over Kelly Ingram and Alabama Power,
through gold Electra's lightning fists
and Linn Park's fountains to the jailhouse
where Blanton waits his verdict, where Cherry
waits for trial. They tissue like smoke
over the interstate, split, descending,
into Fountain Heights, into Oak Hill's graves,
into east-side projects where clothesline billow
and shifts and shirts drift like porters
through the depot's blank. Scatters
spread over Rickwood, over Dynamite Hill
and Tuxedo Junction's boarded jukes,
descending like night herons
into Elmwood where you wait
beneath a stone and a secret name.

*

There are angels. There are angels!
you said. *They guard and watch.*
Tonight, their sudden wings
multiply the city's glitter,
the universe whose stars,
you said, *are writing of the destiny*
of those within the hand of fate.
Tonight, they haunt the ridge
where Vulcan's gauntlets
hold no torch, no iron,
and the streets below where
no dynamite novas bloom.
In abandoned halls, pianos
hold their farewell notes,
radios tremble quietly.
All that is empty is space
like a broken mouth.
A sleep curls there
till the righteous sounds emerge.

Still in Motion

Blear in the burnished air
then wings clap, collapse,
bruise as if some thumb
pressed the sclera of the day.

Dark haunts the punished eye.
Smoke marbles sun.
And every stare can feather
in sudden throngs of pain.

Notes

A *Murmuration of Starlings* is part of an ongoing project to elegize and memorialize the martyrs of the Civil Rights movement, whose names are inscribed on the stone table of the Civil Rights Memorial that stands today outside the Southern Poverty Law Center in Montgomery, Alabama.

"Substantiation" is based on testimony in the trial of J. W. Milam and Roy Bryant for the murder of Emmett Till in 1955. There is no surviving transcript of the trial, but much of it may be reconstructed using the newspaper accounts gathered by Christopher Metress in his volume *The Lynching of Emmett Till: A Documentary Narrative* (University of Virginia Press, 2002). The reporter is based loosely on James L. Hicks of the *Cleveland Call and Post* and conflated with William Bradford Huie, who wrote for *Look*.

In reconstructing the events recalled in "B/W," "The Crowd He Becomes," "For Reverend James Reeb," "A Mumuration of Starlings," and "The Small Birds of Sound," I am indebted to Taylor Branch's Civil Rights trilogy—*Parting the Waters*, *Pillar of Fire*, and *At Canaan's Edge* (Simon and Schuster, 1988, 1998, and 2006)—and as well to Charles E. Fager's *Selma 1965* (Scribner, 1974), Diane McWhorter's *Carry Me Home* (Simon and Schuster, 2001), and Spike Lee's documentary *4 Little Girls* (1997).

Sun Ra, appearing in "B/W," obliquely in "Tuck," and finally in "At Sun Ra's Grave" was a jazz musician, born in Birmingham, who would claim he was from Saturn after moving from Birmingham in 1946 in response to racial difficulties, only a year before a campaign of dynamite bombing of the homes and churches of African Americans began in Birmingham. Much of my treatment of Sun Ra is drawn from his recordings and liner notes, but I am as well indebted to John F. Szwed's *Space Is the Place: The Life and Times of Sun Ra* (De Capo, 1997).

"B/W." The first section, "Out of This World—1946," looks forward to Sun Ra's album *The Magic City* (1965, re-released on Evidence ECD22069), which includes a photograph of the welcome sign. This section also refers to a 1945 film, *Out of This World*, featuring a song of the same title (with lyrics by Johnny

Mercer), sung by the lead Eddie Bracken, using Bing Crosby's voice; the Crosby version is hard to find, but the interested reader may easily discover a version of the song by Ella Fitzgerald, which is recommended listening. The second, third, and fifth sections reference songs that were on the Billboard Top Ten charts the weeks of the bombings in question. "Le Son Ra's 'Hours After' b/w 'Great Balls of Fire'—1958" references a 45rpm single collected on *Sun Ra: The Singles* (Evidence ECD22164–2) and adapts part of a poem included in the liner notes to *Jazz in Silhouette* (1958, re-released on Evidence ECD22012–2). The final section references John Coltrane's recording of "Out of This World" on the 1962 release, *Coltrane* (Impulse! IMPD-215) as well as liner notes from Sun Ra's album *When Angels Speak of Love* (recorded 1963, released 1966, now available on Evidence ECD22216–2).

"Tuck" references, in its second section, Jaybird Coleman's 1927 recording "No More Good Water—'Cause the Pond Is Dry," which may be heard on Document Records DOCD-5140 *Jaybird Coleman & The Birmingham Jug Band (1927–1930)*. The third section of this poem approaches the lyrics to the standard "Bye Bye Blackbird" through several of Coltrane's recordings of it, including the live recording available on the album *Bye Bye Blackbird* (1962, Original Jazz Classics OJCCD-681–2); one might also have in the background, too, Coltrane's "Alabama," available on *Coltrane Live at Birdland* (1963, available on Impulse/MCA MCAD-33109).

"At Sun Ra's Grave" quotes, in its final section, lines from Sun Ra's poem "The Magic City," included with the album *The Magic City* (1965, re-released on Evidence ECD22069). This poem is dedicated to Daniel Alarcón, Diann Blakely, Chris Campagna, and Sun Ra, fellow Alabamians.

Copyright Credits

Other Books in the Crab Orchard Series in Poetry

Muse
Susan Aizenberg

Lizzie Borden in Love:
Poems in Women's Voices
Julianna Baggott

This Country of Mothers
Julianna Baggott

The Sphere of Birds
Ciaran Berry

White Summer
Joelle Biele

In Search of the Great Dead
Richard Cecil

Twenty First Century Blues
Richard Cecil

Circle
Victoria Chang

Consolation Miracle
Chad Davidson

Furious Lullaby
Oliver de la Paz

Names above Houses
Oliver de la Paz

The Star-Spangled Banner
Denise Duhamel

Beautiful Trouble
Amy Fleury

Soluble Fish
Mary Jo Firth Gillett

Pelican Tracks
Elton Glaser

Winter Amnesties
Elton Glaser

Always Danger
David Hernandez

Red Clay Suite
Honorée Fanonne Jeffers

Fabulae
Joy Katz

Train to Agra
Vandana Khanna

If No Moon
Moira Linehan

For Dust Thou Art
Timothy Liu

Strange Valentine
A. Loudermilk

Dark Alphabet
Jennifer Maier

American Flamingo
Greg Pape

Crossroads and Unholy Water
Marilene Phipps

Birthmark
Jon Pineda

Year of the Snake
Lee Ann Roripaugh

Misery Prefigured
J. Allyn Rosser

Roam
Susan B. A. Somers-Willett

Becoming Ebony
Patricia Jabbeh Wesley